PLAYBOOK for Teens

Meet fascinating women in STE@M™
Follow their "plays"
Create your Dream Career

PLAYBOOK
for TEENS

Meet fascinating women in STE@M[TM]
Follow their "plays"
Create your Dream Career

by

Cari Lyn Vinci   Carleen MacKay

Co-authors

A Career Playbook Series
On stage, at work or in sports, a "Playbook" describes strategies to follow to reach new goals.

Printed by CreateSpace, an Amazon Company
Available from Amazon.com, CreateSpace.com and other online stores

Our PLAYBOOK for Teens is dedicated to:

- The smart, talented teenage girls who will become the future business owners and leaders in STE@M industries.

- And, our STEM organization partners whose talent pool problems we help to solve.

What do the future business owners and leaders in STE@M look like?

Old opinion: Girls don't go into STE@M careers

Now opinion: Young women are needed, wanted and VERY successful in STE@M careers.

By looking at the very lovely photos on the next page, can you guess who matches the descriptions below?

- Designs products to replace damaged organs
- Hardware Engineer at a Fortune 100 company
- Engineering Manager in Client Platform Division of Fortune 500 Technology Company
- Has a Masters Degree from Carnegie Mellon University
- Career in Environmental Planning & Management
- An electrical and computer engineer
- A Program Manager for Integrated Computing and STEM education
- Combining an MBA with Math for a high level career
- A Candidate for a PhD in Chemistry with a concentration in Biotechnology.
- A graduate student researcher in Genetics
- A Dental Assistant en route to being a Pediatric Dentist
- A High School Senior loving Art
- A Blacksmith/ Artist
- 2 Business owners, Home Builders
- An Entrepreneur, incubator business owner
- A Strategic Business Development manager
- A Doctorate in Biomedical engineering

Surprised?

Yes, scientists, technology professionals, engineers, artists and math majors today, really do look like that!

Read on to see who is who!

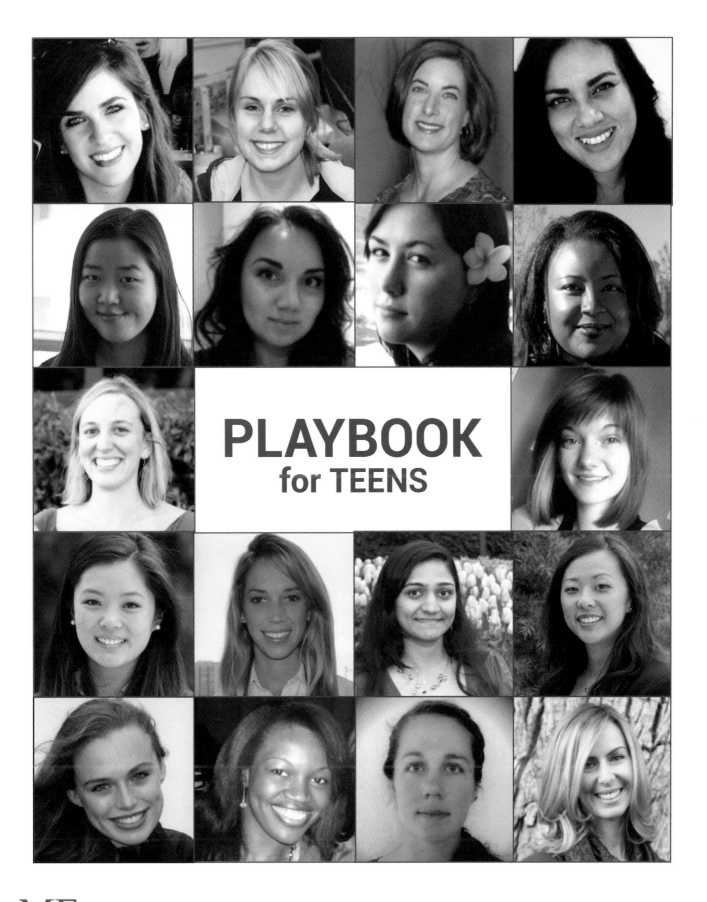

PLAYBOOK
for TEENS

ME,Inc CEO OF MY LIFE

INVINCIBLE
ENTERPRISES

TABLE OF CONTENTS

The Young Women of STE@M[TM]
A Career Playbook Series

Once upon a 20th century time, we prepared our children for the opportunities that century offered the U.S.A.

That was then.

The changed 21st century demonstrates significant shortcomings in preparing teens, especially young women, for the opportunities this century offers the U.S.A.

This is now!

Courtesy of ME, Inc., and directly from the real-life stories of young women who achieved exciting futures in new markets of the 21st century, are new "plays" designed to inspire young women to take charge, to make plans and to become the future business leaders and entrepreneurs; to become "CEO's" of their lives!

The Art of the Start
Introduction to Early Stage Career Planning

So, what does the "art of the start" mean?

It means to imagine your future...

It means to begin to think of your future life and work in the world as it is becoming not as it once was...

It means to listen to the stories of others and connect their stories with your youthful interests...

It means to dream and, as a result of imagining, thinking, listening and dreaming to begin to set a course for your future...

It means that if you connect what's important to you, like the women in these stories demonstrate, with what's important to the emerging world of work, you will make a strong start into the wonderful journey that lies ahead.

And, that, dear girls, is the **"art of the start."**

Carleen MacKay
Co-Author

FOREWORD - About This Playbook

On stage, at work or in sports, a "Playbook" describes strategies to follow to reach new goals. In the theatre, for example, a playbook provides the actors with specific words and actions that are designed to bring the script to life. In football, each player's movements are designed to help score – or prevent – a touchdown.

This is a PLAYBOOK about "Career Sweet Spots" in STE@M careers.

A "Career Sweet Spot" is a recipe for success. It is the intersection of several elements.

- Talents / Skills
- Personality
- Outlook...Market Reality
- Passions / Values
- Investment

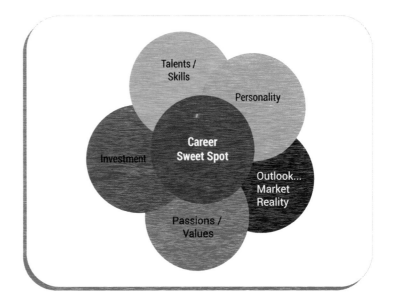

Our "Playbook" is filled with stories of young women ... just a few years older than you are today, who created their "winning game plans" and live in their "Career Sweet Spot."

You will read how they overcame obstacles in their pursuit of new ways to work in a changed time to become CEO's of their lives.

Our storytellers will surprise you with options that you may not know about or could even imagine as part of your tomorrow. As you read, note how their actions (their "plays") prepared them for interesting and successful futures.

You know that STEM stands for – careers in Science, Technology, Engineering and Math. But, do you know what the "A" in STE@M stands for? ART! Yes, ART.... re-imagined.

This is important because art, as you will read, is a key part of the big changes and opportunities made possible by new technologies.

Read on. Fun, fame & fortune are waiting for those who discover their "Career Sweet Spot" in the growing STE@M opportunities!

So let's go.... Full STE@M ahead!

Cari Lyn Vinci
Co-Author and Founder of ME, Inc. USA

A Story about Learning Life's Lessons
A Cinderella Story

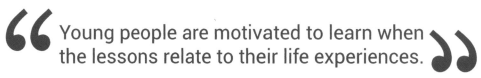

Young people are motivated to learn when the lessons relate to their life experiences.

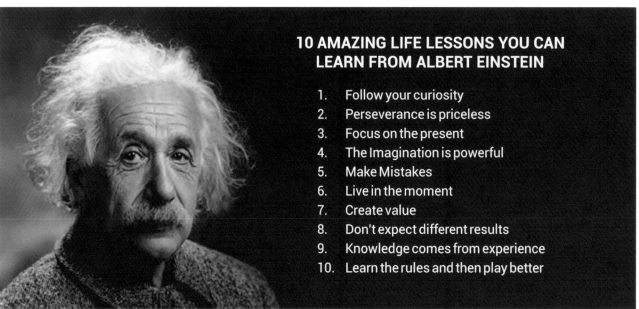

10 AMAZING LIFE LESSONS YOU CAN LEARN FROM ALBERT EINSTEIN

1. Follow your curiosity
2. Perseverance is priceless
3. Focus on the present
4. The Imagination is powerful
5. Make Mistakes
6. Live in the moment
7. Create value
8. Don't expect different results
9. Knowledge comes from experience
10. Learn the rules and then play better

Nicole Chaffee's Story

Once-upon-a-real-time, Nicole was born to a hard-working family of modest means. Her parents didn't hold out the idea that completing college would be a realistic goal for Nicole to achieve. As a result of this early life perspective, her ambitions were limited. In her early years of high school, for example, she had plans to study art and paint pictures on a San Francisco pier. This, however, soon changed.

Like the fictional Cinderella, Nicole's story got much worse before it got better.

While Nicole was in high school, her mother lost a battle with colon cancer. Not surprisingly, this had a profound impact on Nicole.

From her painful life experience and with help from the teacher who took such a high level of interest in her, Nicole began to focus her future on a much bigger goal - finding a cure for colon cancer - the very cancer that had taken her mother's life.

Through grants, school loans, various jobs and a lot of hard, dedicated work; Nicole is now a candidate for a PhD in Chemistry with a concentration in Biotechnology.

Seeing great potential in Nicole, the Director of U.C. Davis' Biotechnology program opened another door. This fairy godmother inspired her to consider "endless career possibilities" where she can use her advanced degree. Nicole is considering applying her knowledge to patent law and even starting her own business. Following her own advice, she has "paid it forward" by opening doors of opportunity for her younger sister and brother who are now college students.

Nicole Chaffee

Ask Yourself:

- What ONE thing did I learn from reading Nicole's story?

- What "plays" did Nicole make that I can use in my PLAYBOOK?

- What lessons is life trying to teach me?

- What can I learn from my life experiences that will help me in the future?

Nicole's Advice:

If I could talk to my teenage self, I'd tell me....

- "Listen to the messages you receive every day. Do what it takes, keep an open mind and listen to people with experience."

- "Find out where the doors to the future are and begin to open them."

My Playbook Journal

A Story about an Artistic Scientist!

Careers in biological science are expected to continue to rank in the top 25 careers by 2020.

The McKinsey Global Institute (one of our favourite resources) recently reported: "As our understanding of the gnomic makeup of humans increases, so does the ability to manipulate genes and improve health diagnostics and treatments."

Place "studied" bets on your future!

Abigail (Abby) Yu's story

Abigail is a graduate student researcher in Genetics at UC Davis. She describes the "cool" things she does at work: "I get to work on plasmodium, the genus of parasitic protozoa responsible for causing malaria, and develop molecular tools for researching it. My work combines both 'wet' and 'dry' lab. I design, create, and test DNA-binding proteins in cells and also develop computer programs to analyse old data in new ways, or analyse new data from newly developed assays."

Sounds like a mouthful of sophisticated information, doesn't it?

Wait...read on for "the rest of Abby's story."

Abby's high school biology teacher had majored in Genetics and instilled the sense of scientific curiosity in her. As a result, at the age of 17 Abby decided to pursue biology instead of her earlier interest ... art.

Role models and mentors surrounded her from the very start. She credits her parents' approval and encouragement, the people who are pursuing similar careers and her lab-mates as her core day-to-day support teams.

We asked Abby what surprises her most about her career. *"The people! Suffice to say, mass media stereotypes of nerds with no social life certainly coloured my view, at least a little. However, as I progress through my graduate career, I am happy to be a part of a community full of wildly intelligent, vivacious, and creative individuals."*

"What's most surprising is that many people recognize and encourage my artistic talents and pursuits. My lab mates come to me for advice on graphic design and I was recently approached to create an illustration for a News and Views article in Nature Methods.

"As a graduate student, I usually set my own hours. The flexibility to design, schedule, and execute my experiments makes balancing work and life easier. I can usually find plenty of time to pursue my hobbies - art and design."

We asked Abby about the challenges and obstacles she has faced and overcome. "I was fortunate enough to live in an environment where the idea of women in science was not only accepted, but was also encouraged. If anything, most of the challenges I faced were from within: my fear of failure, my own high expectations and feeling inadequate.

While these feelings are certainly not unique to me, I've managed to overcome them over the years.

"I still have high expectations for myself, but I've learned not to be so disappointed when I don't meet them. My next hurdle is completing my PhD in Genetics. In a strange way, as I learn more my studies becomes easier and more energizing."

Abby Yu

Ask Yourself:

- What ONE thing did I learn from reading Abby's story?

- What "plays" did Abby make that I can use in my PLAYBOOK?

- Am I willing to dream about changing the world?

- Will I remember that all journeys start with a single step and that, very often, it is the first step that is the hardest?

- Do I have a passion for science?

- Where can I find information on careers in science that are projecting a bright future?

- What organizations can I join to learn more about science careers?

And, we are happy to tell you, our artistic scientist,
Abby helped us design the Playbook layout.
Thank you, Abby!

Abby's Advice:

If I could talk to my teenage self, I'd tell me....

- Do not pigeonhole or isolate yourself and seize opportunities to help others. And do your math homework!

- Keep an open mind. All knowledge is worth having. There is always a need for people who have interdisciplinary training in what some may perceive as disparate fields. People who are capable of synthesizing knowledge across fields to innovate are invaluable.

- Failure is standard fare in science, and my career has forced me to confront and accept it. I've learned that, especially in science, failure is rarely final and is often a valuable learning opportunity.

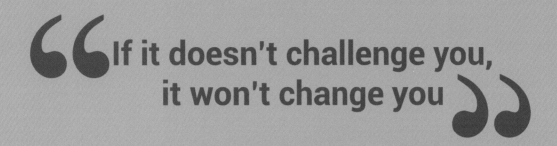

My Playbook Journal

New inventions, innovations and technologies are eliminating many of the "old" ways of doing things. In particular, pay attention to the changing healthcare profession and be receptive to the new opportunities this century offers.

Amanda Straight's story

Amanda is a Dental Assistant whose stated goal is to serve her community and "help people to feel comfortable in the dental chair while improving their dental health."

As Amanda tells it, "When I was young, I liked going to the dentist." What? A positive dental experience? Why it was only last century that a dental visit was as scary as – well, as scary as going to the dentist! What's changed? The answer is ... just about everything!

From new laser procedures, improved diagnostic capabilities because of computer-enhanced images, to recent advances in nanotechnology procedures and major developments in materials for all-ceramic restorations...to gentler, faster processes, just about everything has been made better in a few short years.

What else has changed in dentistry? Well...because of a very large older generation and a very large younger generation, there is no shortage of people to help today and tomorrow. It's a cutting-edge profession and a smart career choice if you are drawn to this work.

Back to Amanda's story in her words: "I never had the desire to go into the field of dentistry until my sophomore year of high school when I visited the Eastland Career Centre in Groveport, Ohio. I noticed that it offered unique opportunities in dentistry that were beyond normal high school classes. I wanted to take full advantage. I worked hard and after studying many hours, I was able to climb to the top of my class and win the SkillsUSA* national competition in dental assisting in 2011.

But that wasn't the end – it was the beginning. I recently graduated from Columbus State Community College with an Associate of Science degree.   At 20, I have a job that allows me to serve my community and help people feel comfortable during dental procedures. I am ready for my next step, to attend Ohio State University's dental college."

When asked about her role models or mentors, Amanda echoed what so many successful women expressed to us. She told us that her parents always pushed her to succeed and praised her for all her successes. She has always looked to them for support. *"Without them, I could not have achieved my goals. I have a stable and secure job. I make great money for a twenty-year old and I live comfortably within my means. I have the satisfaction of knowing that I have accomplished a lot. Sure, I've faced challenges on my way to success; mainly the sacrifice of personal time. I spent a lot of time studying when others were playing and I often wanted to give up.*

But...today I am so thankful that I pushed through those moments and am eager to face the schooling ahead of me in order to become a children's dentist – a dream I have worked hard to achieve."

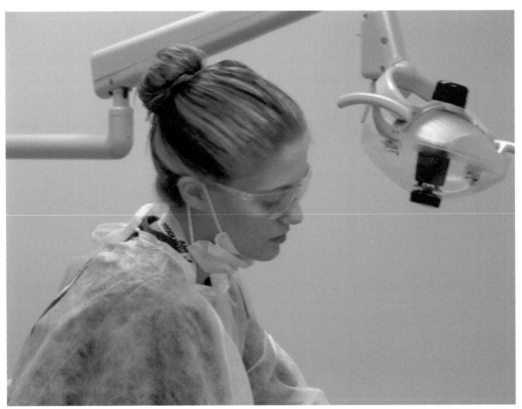

Amanda Straight

Amanda's Advice:

If I could talk to my teenage self, I'd tell me....

- "Helping others and touching their lives is an important goal. Science is such a broad field and it can be applied to so many things. There are girls who are designing new technology that will save lives or eliminate cancer. I cannot express the awesome possibilities within this field. They are innumerable!

- Don't be stopped by the fact that you are a girl."

Ask Yourself:

- What ONE thing did I learn from reading Amanda's story?

- What "plays" did Amanda make that I can use in my PLAYBOOK?

- Does a practical and stable career – one that will thrive in the time of change ahead – meet my needs, interests and goals?

- Does it make sense for me to "take one bite at a time" out of the education these careers require? Taking a "bite" allows me to explore, adjust, earn and grow while learning more about the many options available to me.

- Are there people in the healthcare field who might inspire me by telling me more stories about their work? For example, can I talk with my local dentist or their dental assistant?

- Or, should I ask our family veterinarian about opportunities in their field; or, the local pharmacist about their growing and changing field?

- How can I find out which careers in science fit my unique personality?

- Will I be in my "Career Sweet Spot" with a career in science?

The only difference between stumbling blocks and stepping stones is the way in which we use them

My Playbook Journal

Today, according to Investor's Business Daily, "only 16% of American high school seniors are proficient in mathematics and interested in a STEM [AKA: STE@M] career. At the same time, it is projected that STEM jobs will grow 26% by 2020."

WE MAKE A LIVING BY WHAT WE GET, WE MAKE LIFE BY WHAT WE GIVE
- Sir Winston Churchill

Heidi Espindola's story

Heidi is her early 30's, has completed a Bachelor of Science degree in Physics and Math, a teaching credential and a Master's Degree in Education. Whew!

Heidi is a program manager at the UC Davis Center for Integrated Computing and STEM education.

Her work requires expertise in teaching, education law and practice as well as in computing and robotics technology. She will tell you, as she told us, that her gift to future generations is in imparting this knowledge to people like you. She has combined her gift to others with her more self-focused interest in exploring new scientific discoveries

Heidi's story in her own words: "I work with UC Davis professors and researchers, K-12 teachers and administrators, industry professionals and government personnel to promote the integration of computing and robotics into regular STEM classrooms."

"I never do the same thing from day to day and I am always talking to someone new. I create marketing plans and products, direct teacher professional development, edit curriculum, write contracts and grants, and communicate with our various partners to further our mission of attracting young people to the fastest growing opportunities in the future of America."

We asked Heidi about her role models and mentors and how they influenced her to make the choices. This is what she told us: *"My mother was a strong role model. She was a single mother who completed her MS in mechanical engineering after I was born. Her expectations of me were always high and she never doubted my competency.*

She taught me to be an analytical thinker and to always persevere. She stood up for her ethical and moral beliefs which led me to seek positions where I can advocate for others."

What obstacles did she face? "A lot of the obstacles I have faced have been of my own creation. My biggest challenge was rethinking my first college major. I did some soul searching and realized that my original career choice was not the right fit for me. I then transferred from a 4-year university to a small junior college. I persevered and, looking back on it now, realize that moving to a junior college was the best path for me. It allowed me to explore my options in a less pressured environment. It also allowed me to save a lot of money!"

Heidi Espindola

Ask Yourself:

- What ONE thing did I learn from reading Heidi's story?

- What "plays" did Heidi make that I can use in my PLAYBOOK?

- Am I interested in doing work that will better the lives of others?

- Is it important for me to "Pay it Forward?"

- What can I do today that my future self will thank me for?

Heidi's Advice:

If I could talk to my teenage self, I'd tell me....

- Minimize your college debt. Start in a junior college or by taking college level courses while still in high school.

- Persist. When you get into the job market, you will become an extremely valuable asset to any organization you target. The world will be ready for your talent.

My Playbook Journal

A Story about the Need for Speed

 USA Today recently reported that the focus on 'Getting young women interested and immersed in computer science programs comes at a time when one million new jobs in tech-related fields will be created in the next decade.'

Allison Goodman's story

Allison is a young woman with a talent for stretching her limits. Allison, an electrical and computer engineer at Intel, is a pro at solving new problems by creating new, patentable ideas. She is particularly interested in increasing computer speed to help people connect and share data faster than ever before. To accelerate getting information around the world so it feels instantaneous, Allison creates products that are a combination of writing software programs and electrical components that together try to predict what we want to accomplish with our computer.

Her story began when she started to sort out and prioritize the different things that she found interesting. She tried, but couldn't find that "one thing" that was most important to her. Allison's father helped by telling her he would pay for ONE year of school – but only if she studied engineering. Since this was the only deal offered, she accepted it and left home for college.

Allison came to appreciate her father's wisdom. It helped her become self-reliant. Knowing she had to pay for the balance of college, Allison applied for scholarships and soon discovered that scholarships in engineering were not as difficult to get as she had once thought.

While Allison had initially struggled to find the "one thing" she wanted to do, she now realizes that the opportunity to study hands-on engineering opened her eyes to a number of options that she had never considered. Today, Allison finds challenges and opportunities at Intel. She has been able to change roles every few years and her technical talents have led to positions in project management and customer service.

Imagine. Allison has travelled to 22 countries on behalf of Intel, has met interesting and dynamic people, continues to learn about the world, and finds that new opportunities are always around the next corner. Fantastic!

Allison Goodman

Ask Yourself:

- What ONE thing did I learn from reading Allison's story?

- What "plays" did Allison make that I can use in my PLAYBOOK?

- Is it time to follow the progress of certain organizations' efforts? For example, should I pay attention to big names like Google, Intel or Apple?

- Or, do emerging organizations, standing on the brink to the future, grab my attention?

- Do I have a passion for technology?

- Where can I find information on careers in technology that are projecting a bright future?

- What organizations can I join to learn more about careers in technology?

Allison's Advice:

If I could talk to my teenage self, I'd tell me....

- Get started. Work with what your parents are able to offer you and, remember, you deserve the success you work hard to achieve.

- Don't compare yourself to others; you are unique. Find your own voice!

- Begin to explore leading-edge employers' opportunities because that is where you will find the company of like-minded people with similar goals.

A Story about Beating the Odds

 By 2018 there will be 14 million opportunities that require more than a high school education but less than a bachelor's degree.

WHEN SOMETHING GOES WRONG IN YOUR LIFE, JUST YELL, "PLOT TWIST!", AND MOVE ON

Gina Lujan's story

Gina beat the odds. Her story tells the value of focussing on the future even in the midst of dealing with challenges that seem overwhelming. Gina left home at the age of 14 and became a Mom at 16.

Sound familiar?

It should because, believe it or not, more than half a million teenage girls become mothers every year. Unfortunately, the consequences are usually grim for mothers and their children.

The overwhelming majority of young, teenage mothers end up on welfare. Some find work that pays enough to sustain them and their children and a few overcome the challenges and barriers they face. In most cases, however, the cycle continues and the children find fewer opportunities as a result of their mothers' own tough start in life.

Initially, it appeared that this would be Gina's fate. She began her work life in a sandwich shop then in an auto shop. To better her situation, Gina took a positive first step and completed high school. Success followed. Without any formal education beyond high school, Gina started her first business at 21 and later opened a retail store.

Gina had the guts and resolve to overcome the hurdles she faced. She continued to learn and taught herself web design and basic programming.

Update. As so often happens to people who take charge of their lives, today Gina has created a good life for her family. She is now a mother of six, a wife, a social entrepreneur, a social engineer and a business owner. Gina focussed her career on helping her community. She co-founded the Hacker Lab in Sacramento in 2012. A second Hacker Lab opened recently and Gina is now scouting for additional locations.

What is a Hacker Lab, you ask?

A Hacker Lab provides a community space for programmers, designers and entrepreneurs to *"work individually and collaboratively on cool things like mobile and web applications."* Look around: Hacker Labs are opening through out the country.

P.S. Gina was featured in Sacramento's Business Journal in "Top Execs"   You can read about it at http://bit.ly/1eFTDYd

Business Journals exist in most large cities. Find one in or near your hometown. It will tell you who, what and where work is going on. Some of this work might prove interesting to you.

Gina Lujan

Ask Yourself:

- What ONE thing did I learn from reading Gina's story?

- What "plays" did Gina make that I can use in my PLAYBOOK?

- Am I ready to begin to face the future on its own terms?

- Am I prepared to take inventory of my skills and talents and focus on what I can do and not make excuses for what I can't do?

- Should I visit a Hacker's Lab and meet some of the interesting people working there? They are very likely to have ideas and suggestions for me that I might not otherwise have thought about!

Gina's Advice:

If I could talk to my teenage self, I'd tell me....

- Explore certifications, including online certifications. Employers, clients and customers value these certifications.

- There are great opportunities for people who learn basic programming and other technical skills. The sooner you begin; the sooner you win.

- Push forward; continue to learn and before you know it, you will be in a place where you want to be.

- "Jalal ad-Din Rumi" - Let the beauty of what you love be what you do.

My Playbook Journal

A Story about the Power of Internships

 Does it surprise you that so many of our young women of STE@M see their common bond as achieving that noble goal of improving the lives of others? Do you feel this bond?

Dena Lumbang's Story

Here is a story of relentless pursuit and of using technology to improve her life and the lives of others.

Dena's story began at the age of 13 when her Dad brought home a computer. Hard to believe, but at the time it was rather uncommon to have a PC at home. She asked him who the PC was for and he replied: "It's for you; you just don't know it yet." What a beginning! What a Dad!

The computer worked well for a while and then stopped functioning. Undaunted with the task at hand, Dena decided to fix the PC. Not such an easy thing to do since she worked on the computer without telling her parents and her only help was the manual. Dena read how the PC was put together (at 13, we remind you), dismantled the machine and proceeded to fix it. Dena was suddenly tech savvy. Rebuilding that computer several times gave Dena great confidence.

Fast forward to high school when she attended a Regional Occupational Program. Her first ROP project was to develop a video/program. She finished the project within a week and scored highest in the class.

Her teacher, great mentor that she was, recommended her for an internship at Intel. Even though an internship was a real challenge for a high school student, Dena jumped at the opportunity.

She met these first challenges with the help of two great mentors, her Dad and her ROP teacher. Other role models helped as well. For example, her Aunt helped her to overcome the feeling of being "different" because of her interest in technology as a female and as someone of mixed race.

Does it surprise you that many girls often report feeling inferior to boys in the area of technology when, in fact, there are more girls than boys in the U.S. today? Is it because so many still think of technology as a gender specific gift and are we still suffering from a generational hangover? It doesn't matter why we think thoughts that are not true.

It does matter that we think for ourselves! Think again!

On a roll to a successful future, Dena entered California State University in Sacramento and she was off and running on a straight course to her future.

Not so fast... said life!

Dena was forced to take a leave-of-absence and drop out of college for compelling personal reasons.

Dena managed to overcome her biggest challenge, which was a lack of confidence since she does not have a college degree. How? Dena comments: "I've been lucky enough to get my foot in the door (at Intel) and I continue to learn to improve myself."

Fast forward to Today, Dena is working for Intel as a Strategic Business Development Manager. What does that mean? She researches industries trends. She seeks information on what people are thinking and planning. Because she works with customers on developing new products, she gets to glimpse into the future. She sees "shiny new objects" before they are produced.

Dena described the lifestyle her career provides: "I'm lucky to have a great job at a great company that enables me to work with people worldwide, learn new cultures, and do some travel. There's also flexibility and sometimes I work at home. I have the independence to decide my schedule and priorities as well. I'm entitled to 4 weeks of vacation a year, and every 7 years, I receive a 2 month paid sabbatical. All these benefits and flexibility make it very convenient when I plan vacation and time with my family. Life is hectic with a full time job, a husband, and 3 kids!

What my dad did by bringing that PC home changed my life, and I got into the technology field because I want to change the lives of the next generation with technology that improves lives. "

Dena at Intel Developers Conference

Ask Yourself:

- What organizations (where I want to live) are growing?

- Where can I find out about internships at those that interest me?

- How can I find out which careers in technology fit my unique personality?

- What talents do I have that are important in technology?

- What skills do I need to develop for success in the technology industry?

- Where can I find out which careers in technology are projecting a bright future?

- Will I be in my "Career Sweet Spot" with a career in technology?

Dena's Advice:

- If I could talk to my teenage self, I'd tell me....

- Work...work...work on any issues of self-confidence.

- Look broadly at the field. Being in the technology field doesn't mean you get your hands dirty or sit in front of a computer screen all day every day. Whether innovating healthcare solutions for better patient treatment, improving education worldwide, evolving the entertainment industry, (graphics, marketing) inventing the next big thing (i.e. new wearable's) or creating a new market that exists solely in your mind – technology is where you should be!

- Girls often have a different perspective than boys, regardless of the reasons. In the technology industry, the female point of view is welcomed and needed.

- Be patient and have faith in the future. Make your mistakes, shrug them off and learn from them.

- Don't stop dreaming and don't stop learning. These are your keys to success.

- Get in here and make your mark!

My Playbook Journal

My Playbook Journal

My Playbook Journal

> From siblings to grandparents, family members can teach, influence, and offer words of wisdom. All can impact your life, but none are more important than parents who do their best every day to help their children find their way in this changing world.

5 Lessons in Life from Dr. Seuss

1. Today you are You, that is truer than true. There is no one alive who is Youer than You.
2. Why fit in when you were born to stand out?
3. You have brains in your head. You have feet in your shoes. You can steer yourself any direction you choose.
4. Be who you are and say what you feel, because those who mind don't matter and those who matter don't mind.
5. Today I shall behave, as if this is the day I will be remembered.

Jeni Lee and Maelene Wong's story

Jeni and Maelene knew from an early age they loved science and math. They credit their parents with identifying and actively nurturing their youthful interests.

Jeni's father owned a fibre optics company. He was a busy man who always found time to help Jeni when she wanted to learn how to fix things. Once, when a toy broke, her dad gave her a tool kit and patiently helped her learn how to use it. Armed with new skills and tools, Jeni soon took unbroken toys apart and put them back together because she wanted to learn "how things worked." She learned to experiment and to take risks. In this process, Jeni learned that failing the first time was okay – it was part of the learning process. This early hands-on learning helped Jeni in many ways. She developed problem-solving skills, she gained confidence, she learned patience and it fed her creative curiosity.

Maelene's parents taught her to ask questions and to find her own answers to the challenges she encountered. As immigrants without the luxury of higher education, they impressed upon her the importance of an advanced degree and did everything in their power to ensure all opportunities were available to her. Maelene's parents always offered suggestions while encouraging her to be a self-learner. In doing this, Maelene discovered that she had two passions: she liked to build things and to help people. Bioengineering offered her the opportunity to do both.

Jeni and Maelene met in graduate school at U.C. Davis while earning doctoral degrees in Biomedical engineering. They discovered that they had both graduated from U.C. Berkeley's Bioengineering program, only at different times. Both found that studying was easier, more inspiring and fun when what they learned was directly related to their areas of interest.

Their first advice to students who face a lengthy course of study is to "plow through the basics" and experience the truth. "Advanced learning becomes a gift you give yourself."

Fast-forward a few years. Maelene and Jeni recently formed a business with one of their professors: ViVita Technologies, Inc. Their goal is to design products to replace damaged organs and tissues. Their first task is to demonstrate that their research and work will save patients by providing them with long-lasting heart valve replacements.

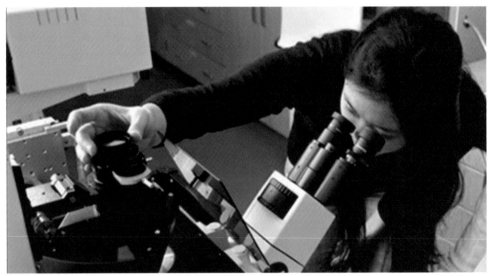

Jeni Lee

Maelene and Jeni's Advice:

If I could talk to my teenage self, I'd tell me....

- Take as many opportunities to learn as possible.

- Stay open, become well rounded, learn history and languages.

- Learn to trust yourself. Pay attention to your intuition and gut.

- Follow your heart. Don't let anything stop you from reaching your dream.

- If others try to discourage you, believe in yourself. You are just as smart as anybody else. Speak out...don't be afraid to be the smart kid.

Photo credits: UC Davis College of Engineering

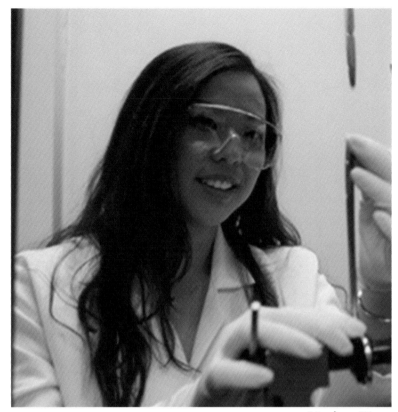

Maelene Wong

Ask Yourself:

- What ONE thing did I learn from reading Maelene and Jeni's story?

- What "plays" did Maelene and Jeni make that I can use in my PLAYBOOK?

- Does my family tree include role models whose lives or work inspire me?

- Who, in my family – old, young or in-between – do I admire and why? Can I find out about their journeys and share my dreams with them?

- Like Jeni and Maelene, what ambitions do I have that can help others?

Photo credits: UC Davis College of Engineering

My Playbook Journal

A Story about a Formula for Success

 While there is no single formula for success, we do know that it will take all of us, learning and working together, to build a future as different from the past as the modern jet and drone are to the horse and buggy of a scant 100 years ago.

Formula for success

1. Have a Dream
2. Believe in Yourself
3. Learn how to make the Dream come True
4. Develop a Plan of Action
5. Make a Commitment to Never, Ever Quit
6. Take Consistent and Massive Action Until the Dream is Reality

Lisa Depew's story

Lisa is an Engineering Manager in the Intel Corporation's Business Client Platform Division and a WOW of a role model.

Listen as we paraphrase how Lisa describes her work: *I work with brilliant people who have a passion for technology and for helping others. We make technology usage more efficient and secure. The goal is to provide people with more time to spend with their families, to learn, grow and innovate.*

At Intel, we look to successful women who are a few steps ahead of us in the world-of-work to mentor and advocate for us. We do the same for girls just beginning to emerge in the STEM field of work.

Let's back up a bit and look at Lisa as a young girl. Lisa didn't come from a "techie" family and didn't even know what engineering was until she was about 15. It was one of her mother's friends who, upon observing that Lisa was good at math, advised her to look into engineering. Lisa did. Just one comment from a trusted adult gave Lisa a career direction.

The University years: The problem-solving mindset of engineering really suited Lisa throughout her university years. Plus, she saw the opportunity to do good things for the world in this career field. Lisa ultimately went on to receive her B.S. in Electrical Engineering from the University of Dayton – just before the 20th Century clock turned to the 21st Century. For the record, she noted a few of the "good things" she knows engineers can do for humanity, and she shares these thoughts with you : "*It's helpful to have someone connect the dots on all the ways engineers help the world. From improving the quality of and access to drinking water, to making car restraint systems safer, to writing software applications that help people track weather and harvest crops, to building prosthetic limbs that help amputees. Engineering makes a world of difference to Society.*"

Fast forward to today at Intel, Lisa's own words: *"Philanthropy and helping others have always been at the core of what matters to me. At Intel, the infrastructure, intellectual capital and resources exist which enable me to do that on an amazingly broad scale. Intel's Corporate Mission is 'this decade we will create and extend computing technology to connect and enrich the lives of every person on earth'.*

I find myself having the greatest impact with my conversation and written communication skills and my ability to connect with others. These are the 'soft skills' that make the brilliant technical ideas come to fruition."

We asked Lisa to describe the lifestyle her career provides. She replied: *"Engineering certainly affords a level of comfort, finance-wise. Part of the reason I chose this career was financial security. I wanted a house and kids and to be able to travel. I've achieved that. What I didn't expect was how much I would travel the world for work. I've been to China, Taiwan, Japan, Malaysia, Israel, Germany, Kenya, Costa Rica, and all over the United States with Intel. I've met and built relationships with colleagues from so many cultures. It's been fascinating learning about their traditions, what concerns them and how they approach problem-solving. Diversity definitely helps us build better products, and learning from the people around us -- classmates, coworkers, family, and friends -- helps engineers develop the best solutions possible."*

As with our other stories about STE@M achievers, Lisa has benefited from the lives of several role models. Two stand out. The first role model was a working mother and technical leader at Intel who inspired Lisa and helped her navigate key career decisions. Lisa followed in her footsteps by winning the Society of Women Engineers' Emerging Leader Award (www.swe.org). Lisa met her second mentor and sponsor when traveling on an Intel service assignment. Both were sent to Kenya to teach computer literacy in remote regions of Africa.

Lisa Depew with children in Kenya

Ask Yourself:

- What ONE thing did I learn from reading Lisa's story?

- What "plays" did Lisa make that I can use in my PLAYBOOK?

- Am I ready to take the first step on my journey towards my future?

- Can I begin by finding teachers, parents, grandparents, aunts, uncles, cousins, brothers, sisters or friends who can share advice and ideas with me about STE@M careers that fit my talent and interests?

- And, if I believe I am ready for a second step, can I seek a mentor who might be a long-term advisor during continued exploration of opportunities and options that suit me?

Lisa's Advice:

If I could talk to my teenage self, I'd tell me....

- Preparation is like the conditioning you have to do to play sports. I remember playing volleyball, we had to run laps, do jump squats, and run drills. We were always thinking, "when do we get to play the game?!?!" Conditioning is critical if you want to play the game in sports or in engineering. You need to take the classes, learn the building blocks, and speak the language. The point is that you need to do the conditioning so that when the time comes, you are ready to play with the best of players.

- A STEM career is a marathon, not a sprint. School is hard, but you can do it. And when you have that degree plus those building blocks—there's nothing you can't accomplish!!!

- Be Brilliant and know that it's OK to be Brilliant. Don't limit yourself. Embrace the gifts and talents that make you uniquely, specially, beautifully you. Be empowered, and share those gifts with the world. And yes, it's okay if you are thought of as "nerdy." Cause smart girls ROCK!

My Playbook Journal

My Playbook Journal

My Playbook Journal

Adrienne Huffman's story

This story tells the tale of a curious young girl who found that computer engineering and electrical engineering both challenged her curiosity. What to do? She graduated from Florida A&M University with two degrees: a B.S. in Electrical Engineering and a B.S. in Computer Engineering. Then, she topped off her Bachelor's degrees with an M.S. in Electrical Engineering from Iowa State.

In college, Adrienne was active with the National Society of Black Engineers. They provided encouragement and a venue to develop her leadership skills. Adrienne was inspired by members of Delta Sigma Theta Sorority, an organization she later joined. Adrienne identifies with the motto of Dr. Paulette Walker, the 25th National President of Delta Sigma Theta Sorority, "No one can make you feel inferior without your consent."

Powerful words of inspiration to young women who, in addition to their commitment to academic learning, must develop strong senses of self-worth in order to reach their goals.

Adrienne's academic interests developed along the way. She, like so many people, began pursuit of a career in computer engineering but found that her interests shifted as she learned. Early influences included her parents who taught her the valuable lessons she lives by today. Notably, they taught her *"in order to achieve success, you have to continue to push through hard moments."* They also taught her that *"with God, anything is possible"* and it was this strong, equal measure of faith and hard work that helped her to see the other side of the high mountain she chose to climb.

Today, Adrienne is a Hardware Engineer at a Fortune 100 company. Her career has rewarded her with a very comfortable lifestyle even as hard work continues to challenge her. She is very active in community focused, professional organizations, and travels frequently. She takes some time and money for herself and enjoys shopping as a self-directed reward strategy. Many wise people believe that it is this balance of learning, working hard, giving and taking that is the most powerful argument for achieving a life well lived.

Adrienne Huffman

Ask Yourself:

- Do I have a passion for engineering?

- Where can I find information on careers in engineering that are projecting a bright future?

- What organizations can I join to learn more about careers in engineering?

- How can I find out which careers in engineering fit my unique personality?

- What talents do I have that are important in engineering?

- What skills do I need to develop for success as an engineer?

- Will I be in my "Career Sweet Spot" with a career in engineering?

Adrienne's Advice:

If I could talk to my teenage self, I'd tell me....

- While working with guidance counselors, place in checkpoints to reevaluate where you are and recalibrate goals as needed. Taking the time to assess where you are on your path is important and can help in providing better direction to your course.

- Expect that some of your plans will change either because your desires change or because of external influences. Life is not linear; so don't expect your life-plans to be either.

- The only person that can hold you back from achieving success is YOU! While it is true that pursuing a STEM career is hard, it is also true that it is only as hard as you make it. In fact this truth applies to any career path. As long as you can overcome any mental blockers that arise, you can disregard naysayers and achieve success.

My Playbook Journal

A Story about Reaching Across Borders of Time and Place

 New opportunities await smart countries and smart people who place their bets on their version of the future. The winners will be those who listen and prepare as the doors to global competitiveness are opening wider by the minute.

Hiral Shah's story

Hiral grew up in India and, as a very young girl; liked doing puzzles and building things. Seeing Hiral's interests and abilities, her uncle and cousin pointed out the similarities between deciphering complex puzzles, building things and solving engineering problems. They advised her that an engineering degree would offer her financial independence and a range of opportunities that she might not otherwise experience.

In large part because of their encouragement, Hiral grew increasingly excited about a career in engineering and studied science, math and basic computer programming in high school.

Hiral's studies paid off when she ranked 9th in a technical competition of 200,000 students.   It was then that her parents joined the other relatives in encouraging her to pursue higher education.

She successfully hurdled her first challenge when she received an engineering degree in India.

Remember her influential cousin? The same cousin "pushed" her towards an advanced degree like he had achieved in the U.S. He explained that would substantially increase her opportunities as well as her income.

However, convincing her parents to send her to the U.S. for an advanced degree was not easy. After all, she was a girl and going off to study in a foreign country far from home would subject her to all sorts of unknowns. Ultimately, her parents realized that she should seize the opportunity and supported her in her pursuit of a Master's Degree at Carnegie Mellon University.

The transition from India to the US was tough. Hiral was lonely and painfully missed the blessings of daily family interaction. Furthermore, her studies were challenging, her advisor was tough. She often felt like giving up and going home. Sometimes, it seemed she endured simply to honour her commitment to her family as well as to herself.

Today, she is appreciative of the struggle because...guess what? Apple Computer recruited her for a very exciting early career opportunity. She describes herself as "super happy" solving new puzzles that matter! She embraces the philosophy of finding new ways to do things as part of her definition of success.

Hiral recommends becoming active in professional organizations. She even launched a Women in Technology group at the Fortune 100 company where she currently works.

There are many organizations for women in technology. Take a look at just two of your choices:

WITI's mission is to empower women worldwide to achieve unimagined possibilities and transformations in economic prosperity. WITI works to ensure that women are fully represented in the influential world of information technology and computing. Go to: www.witi.org.

The National Center for Women & Information Technology works to correct the imbalance of gender diversity in technology and computer. Go to: www.ncwit.org.

Hiral Shah

Ask Yourself:

- What ONE thing did I learn from reading Hiral's story?

- What "plays" did Hiral make that I can use in my PLAYBOOK?

- Am I listening to smart people who are involved in my areas of interest? Should I begin by asking my teachers for their input or by joining a technical club at my high school?

- How about a trip to an Apple store or Verizon or Best Buy in my city? Will conversations with working Techies offer me new insights?

- Should I pay attention to future-focused research by institutions such as MIT, Harvard, Stanford, Carnegie Mellon and others whose business it is to teach me about the future of STE@M?

- Check out: MIT's Technology Review (www.technologyreview.com)

- Harvard Business Review (www.harvard.edu/HBR)

Hiral's Advice:

If I could talk to my teenage self, I'd tell me....

- Don't be afraid of the engineering stereotype; a "geeky guy" who sits in front of a computer all day. That is not a true picture of the real world. Be confident; there are equally smart women in the real world of business.

- Push harder, work on projects outside of school. Take more risks. Try different things.

- Explore internships. They will offer you a strong advantage over other candidates when you are looking for work.

- Develop the soft skills...communication, teamwork, and collaboration with others.

My Playbook Journal

A Story about Opening a Once-Closed Door

 There is a premium on scientific and technical knowledge in today's workplace. This means there in huge opportunity behind that once closed door. Women who master either – or both – will have choices on how, where and when they will work; while earning significant pay for their contributions.
Doors are opening! Come on in!

Uki Dele's story

Uki grew up in Nigeria and, as a young girl, didn't like math. Of course, it didn't matter because Uki was told that -- as a girl -- she didn't need to know math. In fact, she wasn't challenged to learn anything technical and was told to study the social sciences. At 14, Uki studied what her parents and society told her to study. The doors open to her future were ones she did not wish to enter.

California here we come...a journey of over 6000 miles! Imagine the chances her family took, and the changes they all experienced, when they relocated to that extraordinary and strange land – California. Scary, huh? But, it was as the result of this life-changing move that new doors began to open for everyone in the family.

Uki enrolled in Consumes River Community College in Northern California where she took a course in beginning algebra. She was given practical examples and saw how Math applied to life and, what's more, discovered that she was GOOD at the subject. The door to opportunity opened wider when she shot to the top of her class and was asked to tutor other students.

Could anything be better than this? Might she consider teaching math as a profession? Wait a minute.

Perhaps there were other careers to consider; careers whose doors had once been shut tight to this young girl from Nigeria.

She explored, listened and learned. At a career panel, she heard a panelist tell of digging wells and teaching hygiene in emerging countries. This was a defining moment. Uki knew she wanted to combine her interest in math with a focus on the environment. She realized she could help others by solving environmental challenges.

During her undergraduate years she studied civil engineering and was a founding member of the local chapter of "Engineers without Borders" – a group whose cause is doing good for others. Upon completion of her Master's Degree in Environmental Planning and Management, Uki has a "Portfolio career." She works for Washington Suburban Sanitary Commission and is also an instructor at Colorado Technical University.

EWB - USA supports community - driven development programs worldwide. Thousands of members work with communities to find solutions for water supply, sanitation, energy, agriculture, civil works, structures and information systems.

Uki Dele

Uki's Advice:

If I could talk to my teenage self, I'd tell me....

- Relax! Everything is going to be better than I can imagine.

- Invest in a strong foundation. Invest in yourself.

- Develop your critical thinking and problem solving skills.

- With a degree in engineering, I can do anything I want to do.

- Look for role models. My instructor at Consumes Community College was like a 'godfather' to me. He made introductions and taught me the gentle art of mentoring.

- Don't get so caught up with social networking that you lose sight of what is right in front of you. See and learn from each day!

- If you can get through school without loans, do it! Apply for scholarships and get a job that provides education assistance to reduce your out of pocket expenses.

Ask yourself:

- What one thing did I learn from reading Uki's story?

- Did Uki make any "plays" that I can use for my own playbook?

- Where can I learn more about careers in math?

My Playbook Journal

A Story about Releasing the Artist Within

"One of today's biggest lessons is: individuals who create careers that embrace the ongoing advances in technology will succeed.
For example, in a global community without a common language, images are becoming ever more important communication tools. As new technologies provide visual artists more range, imagine the possibilities they offer to enhance storytelling, branding, advertising, and marketing.
The opportunity for creative artists has never been greater.
The "Creatives" are the "A" in STE@M! "

Charlie Boyle's story

As a high school senior, Charlie is an early starter and isn't waiting for college to begin preparing for her life/work.

Since her earliest years, Charlie has been an avid reader, an accomplished writer and an artist. She excels in both the classroom and in competitive sports. Over six feet tall, Charlie is a prime candidate for an athletic career. But when she thinks about her future, it is writing and drawing that speak to her.

In her junior year of high school, Charlie began to focus on how to best use her talents in the modern workplace. In her senior year she was offered a basketball scholarship from a college with a solid academic program in her desired area. Because she is planning for her future and works hard on the court, Charlie will get the education she wants without having to take on the burden of student loans.

Charlie anticipates pursuing a marketing management degree that will integrate her writing skills and talent for artistic composition. Even if she changes direction later, she knows that multi-media skills will be valuable in any STE@M industry. Since Charlie has completed most of her core high school work, she is now taking online courses in technology. Charlie is focussed and purposeful. She is on her way.

Charlie Boyle

Ask Yourself:

- What ONE thing did I learn from reading Charlie's story?

- What "plays" did Charlie make that I can use in my PLAYBOOK?

- If creative artists are changing the world of advertising, marketing, entertainment, education, sales and business itself, how can I use my artistic creativity to reach my unique, very personal life goals?

- What skills/education do I need to combine art & STEM into a career that will support the lifestyle I want?

Charlie's Advice:

If I could talk to my teenage self, I'd tell me....

- If you can't do what you were born to do, you won't become who you are meant to be. Combine your interests with the skills the workplace demands; your future will thank you.

- You know you are going to need certain skills to pursue your dreams. Why wait for college? Begin now. Take classes and learn the "4 C's" – Critical Thinking, Communications, Creativity & Collaboration. If you learn these early, you'll be ahead of the crowd.

- When in the early stages of reaching for your future career, take opportunities to learn, explore options and get some real-life experience.

STEM TO STE@M

Where Art and Design meets Science, Technology, Engineering and Mathematics

My Playbook Journal

A Story about Playing with FIRE

 According to the U.S. Bureau of Labor Statistics, demand for Metal Fabricators is expected to grow between 18% and 22% through 2020.

Mackenzie O'Brien's story

Mackenzie is a Fabricator and Blacksmith. "What I think is cool about my work is that I get to play around with fire."

As she tells it, "I first got interested in working with metal in high school; I must have been around 15 years old when I started buying jewelry pieces to make wire necklaces and earrings. When I turned 21, I wanted to work on a larger scale. That required knowledge of how to use and manage heat to shape thicker metal."

Mackenzie spent several years as an apprentice, developing her skills in different blacksmith shops. When it came time to start working, she was not needed full time by any one blacksmith. So, she worked a few part-time jobs. Mackenzie traveled to different shops and learned from several smiths who had different skills sets and interests. Then, to multiply her value, she studied welding and machining classes at community college.

Fast forward. Today Mackenzie uses a combination of sophisticated technology and blacksmithing skills. Her mix of artistry, technical knowledge, skills and collaboration helps her create work that is unique and high quality. Additionally, she also makes tools for fireplaces and artistic driveway security gates that blend visual appeal and durability. She is a true artist.

What sets Mackenzie apart is her big picture vision. Rather than give up because she couldn't find a full-time job, she recognized that several part-time jobs provided a great opportunity to broaden her skills. Mackenzie blazed her own trail, here is her portfolio career.

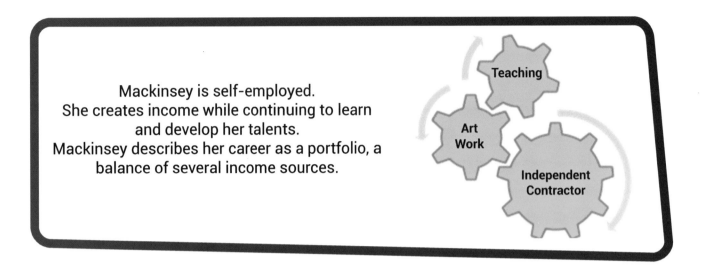

Mackinsey is self-employed.
She creates income while continuing to learn and develop her talents.
Mackinsey describes her career as a portfolio, a balance of several income sources.

Teaching

Art Work

Independent Contractor

Note that all aspects of the portfolio play to her skills, her strengths and her interests. At any given time, the balance of the portfolio can shift and, of course, the sources of income will shift as well.

The bottom line is that Mackenzie runs her career as a business, allowing for fluctuations in the market and seasonal variances. Big words, huh? The simple meaning is Mackenzie is prepared to fill-in other sources of work during expected or unexpected changes.

While maintaining a portfolio career, she is working to complete additional certifications to increase her "toolbox" of skills. To achieve this goal, she takes classes in different types of welding, including Gas Metal Arc Welding (GMAW) plus completing additional computer-aided online learning.

What are some of the advantages of Mackenzie's approach?

1.   She works for herself.
2.   She diversifies her sources of income.
3.   She invests in herself by continuing to learn.
4.   She keeps ahead of prospective changes in the market.
5.   She does what she "loves".

In a profession where there are few women blacksmiths, we asked Mackenzie to tell us about her mentors, advisors and role models. Blacksmiths from North Carolina, Wisconsin and California played active roles in teaching Mackenzie and encouraging her early passion for metalwork. As you might expect, most were men; although she just finished a project with a well-known female blacksmith. Unlike her mentors, her family and friends initially laughed off her ambitions. They are not laughing now!

Mackenzie's hard-earned skills have paid off while, at the same time, she freely admits that machining, welding and blacksmithing has taken a toll on her body. This fact alone may change the balance of her portfolio career at some point-in-time.

Mackenzie O'Brien (R)

Ask Yourself:

- What ONE thing did I learn from reading Mackenzie's story?

- What "plays" did Mackenzie make that I can use in my PLAYBOOK?

- Am I exploring all my options from the perspective of who I am and what I like to do?

- Do I have a passion for art?

- Where can I find information on careers in art that are projecting a bright future?

- What organizations can I join to learn more about careers in art and STEM?

- What talents do I have that are important in art?

- What skills do I need to develop for success in an art career?

Mackenzie's Advice:

If I could talk to my teenage self, I'd tell me....

- This is a field that requires a lot of stamina and energy. It is perfect if you like/need variety, physically demanding and "sweaty" work.

- Consider getting a certificate in a trade before going to a community or 4-year college. Certifications allow the time to work on your future before you invest in advanced studies that will take a bigger bite out of your pocketbook.

- If you like machine technology, consider taking a two-year machine technology degree. It will help you choose between several fields; from building ships, planes and automobiles to designing unique artwork. There are opportunities everywhere.

My Playbook Journal

**EVEN IF YOU ARE ON THE RIGHT TRACK,
YOU'LL GET RUN OVER IF YOU JUST SIT THERE**

— WILL ROGERS

My Playbook Journal

A Story about Building on Transferable Skills

Q. Who says math is important?
A. Employers and workplace analysts.
Q: Where do U.S teenagers rank internationally in math skills?
A: American 15 year-olds are below average, ranking 36th out of the 65 countries in the survey.
Q: Do you see an incredible opportunity in these numbers?
A: For some people, although not enough, the opportunities are loud and clear.

Katherine and Rachel Bardis' story

Join us as we visit Rachel & Katherine, cousins and partners in their own land development & home building business. But...oh, what a trip it has been!

Katherine and Rachel come from a family whose business is home-building. Initially, neither considered this business for themselves. From the age of ten, Katherine wanted to be an attorney and went to law school. Rachel got her degree in finance and business economics. They tried careers in classic business settings and discovered that they "didn't like working in cubicles." Since they were gifted with strong doses of headstrong individuality, innovation and self-discovery, they struggled in overly structured work environments.

To be true to themselves, they quit their jobs and formed their own business (yes... building homes). However, they make the point that the degrees they hold have come in handy. Katherine is able to draft and review the company's legal documents, Rachel handles all the financial matters. This puts their skills to work and saves them a lot of money.

So... where once they were the learners in the male-dominated building industry, today they are taking leadership roles. They are teaching classes for industry veterans, bringing "the old boys network" into the new age of technology.

Some of their accomplishments include building unique homes that are accommodating to all ages and stages of life. Looking to the future, they have their eyes set on bringing some old, dilapidated structures back to life to be used as multiple purpose buildings.

Katherine and Rachel have a true passion for building and developing and share this love of creating with those who want to have FUN while working hard. They point out there is a need for a variety of talents in this field: "Just look at what goes into building your favorite shopping mall. It takes creativity, great design, lighting, engineering, architecture, space planning, public relations, marketing, physical labour, colour, and more. Combine these forward-thinking talents and you can expect to create shopping experiences that are awesome."

They enjoy the continued satisfaction of looking at what they build and of laying claim to the fact that many innovations and changes were created by them.

Katherine Bardis (L) and Rachel Bardis (R)

Rachel & Katherine's Advice:

If I could talk to my teenage self, I'd tell me....

- Take your time, figure out what you want to do, there is no rush to grow up.
- Develop a no-quit attitude. Once you decide to do something, find the resources and do it full-board.

Ask Yourself:

- What ONE thing did I learn from reading Katherine and Rachel's story?
- What "plays" did Katherine and Rachel make that I can use in my PLAYBOOK?
- How can I find out which careers using math fit my unique personality?
- Will I be in my "Career Sweet Spot" with a career that incorporates math?
- What change do I want to create in the world?
- Do I want to make that change by forming my own business?
- What can I build to help people and make a lasting mark?

My Playbook Journal

My Playbook Journal

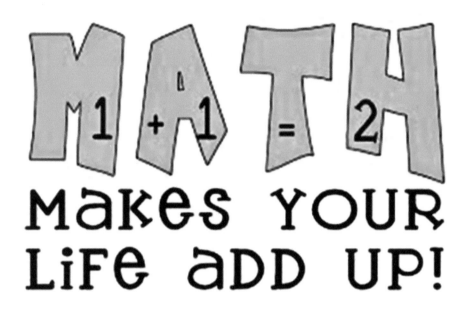

Dana Hoffmann's story

Dana is pursuing an M.B.A. at Harvard, after earning a Bachelor and Master degrees from Santa Clara University. Her goal is to contribute to the entrepreneurial efforts of technology teams. Were Dana's accomplishments easily gained? On the contrary!

Dana has quite a story. "During my Masters degree in Applied Math, I was WAY behind all of the savvy engineers. As one of the only females in the class, I often felt bad about asking simple questions. I also had a packed schedule; going to school from 7am - 9am and working from 9:30am - 8pm to support the high cost of tuition. I received some very low grades during my first year and had to learn how to ask for help. I did, and every weekend I took the opportunity to be tutored by my professors and other students."

But...wait a minute. Go back a few years and see the rest of her tough life struggle. Her Dad died when she was 2 years old and her Mom was left with 3 young girls to raise. As a result, Dana knew from an early age that she'd have to help pay her way through what would be a very expensive education. She accomplished this goal by working and going to school at the same time. It's a tough combination, but one that Dana highly recommends.

On the fortunate side of life, Dana's mom was, and is, a fantastic role model. She is an accomplished scientist, worked for the Secretary of the Interior, was a Professor at MIT and is currently editor-in-chief of SCIENCE magazine. To see her work, go to: **www.sciencemag.org.**

What do Rachel, Katherine and Dana have in common? They continue to persist, overcome and succeed by meeting life's challenges head-on. Challenges that overwhelm and stop so many others.

They all started along one path and then switched careers to take advantage of different, new opportunities. For example, Dana originally worked in corporate finance (forecasting and budgeting) but moved toward the tech side of the business once she attained a M.S. in Applied Math. You may recall that Rachel and Katherine radically changed their careers from the corporate world to the independent world of entrepreneurs. And all three were fortunate to have family members who demonstrated, rather than declared, the value of working for yourself.

P.S. Dana added that she wished she had a ME, Inc. program before starting her education ;-)

Dana Hoffmann

Dana's Advice:

If I could talk to my teenage self, I'd tell me....

- Take your time, figure out what you want to do. There is no rush to grow up.
- Develop a no-quit attitude. Once you decide to do something, find the resources and do it full-board.
- Pick a school based on the major you want, not the location or what the campus looks like.

Ask Yourself:

- What ONE thing did I learn from reading Dana's story?
- What "plays" did Dana make that I can use in my PLAYBOOK?
- What can I do that satisfies me and is needed in the workplace?
- Do I have a passion for math?
- What talents do I have that are important in math?
- What skills do I need to develop for success in a math career?
- Where can I find out which careers in math are projecting a bright future?
- What organizations can I join to learn more about careers in math?

My Playbook Journal

How I see math word problems:

If you have 4 pencils and I have 7 apples, how many pancakes will fit on the roof?
Purple, because aliens don't wear hats.

My Playbook Journal

AFTERWORD .... A common thread

The Playbook Role Models told their stories and shared heart-felt advice. We offered you the first step to write your playbook— inspiration and food for serious thought about your future and the amazing opportunities and possibilities that exist.

Although the young women you read about come from diverse backgrounds and were born with various talents, dreams and personalities, they share several important characteristics.

First, they look at life as a year round school. They embrace the role of "student" beyond their formal education. Committed to growth, these ladies are aware and open to the possibilities the world offers.

Second, they understand that success is not fast or easy. Failure at the beginning is common and they used early "unsuccessful outcomes" as part of the learning process. They said YES to opportunities and added life experiences to their playbook of skills.

Third, these young women took responsibility. They understand, "IT'S UP TO ME TO CREATE THE LIFE I WANT TO LIVE." Based on a future they dreamed of, they developed the skills necessary to take control and design the lives they want.

And, existing resources didn't determine their success. They succeeded because they believed in themselves. It was their courage, willingness and determination that led them to be exceptional rather than average.

What do windshield wipers, fire escapes, Kevlar for bullet-proof vests, spandex, solar heated homes and chocolate chip cookies all have in common? All were invented by women! What fabulous contribution will you give to the world?

Helen Keller said: "Life is either a daring adventure or nothing at all." Our hope is that you will choose to live your life as a daring adventure.

Cari Lyn Vinci & Carleen MacKay

Game On....Your turn to PLAY!

If you start *now* YOU'LL START SEEING RESULTS one day earlier than if you start tomorrow

Ready to PLAY? Here are your next steps:

- Answer the Playbook questions. It's the beginning of a personalized life/career plan and helps determine your "Career Sweet Spot."

- Join us at MEIncUSA.com.

- Request to be part of our BETA testing and get FREE access to our Color Personality Assessment. The assessment will help you determine your "Career Sweet Spot."

Go ahead: unleash your talents, explore your potential, and see how high you can soar.

Become "CEO of my life"... the world is awaiting your Brilliance!

About Us

Cari Lyn Vinci
CEO of my Life
Founder, InVINCIble Enterprises

Cari Lyn Vinci is founder of InVINCIble Enterprises, an organization designing digital products to empower smart, talented teenage girls to become our future business leaders and entrepreneurs. In production is ME, Inc. It provides Role Models, a Game Plan and Mentoring to encourage teens to enter thriving careers in STE@M industries.

Cari is a serial entrepreneur. As president of FranNet West, she coached adults to become the CEO's of their lives. She has hired and motivated over 700 sales consultants, designed training programs, written a book on meeting management, and founded Team da Vinci, a Commercial Division of Keller Williams Real Estate.

This Playbook is "part of the start" of ME, Inc. USA

Carleen McKay
Emergent Workforce Expert U.S.

Carleen is a nationally recognized keynoter, panellist and new product and service developer for clients in all sectors of the economy. She specializes in helping the multi-generational workforce understand the emergent century workplace and adjust their planning in order to meet the demands of a structural shift as unlike any changes the country has experienced in the past half century.

Author or co-author of five books on behalf of workers, Carleen's most recent work includes co-authoring Live Smart after 50 and a series of half a dozen similar Playbooks for all demographics and generations that are either working in – or planning to work in – the U.S. workplace.

"Dream BIG, plan well,
work hard, smile always
and good things will happen"

Cari@MEIncUSA.com
916.220.2830
MEIncUSA.com
http://youtube/G0kFkI7rbcc

My Playbook Journal

I can.
I will.
End of story.

CPSIA information can be obtained at www.ICGtesting.com
Printed in the USA
LVIW01n1305160517
534718LV00003B/18